iPhone 7 for seniors

Simplified iPhone 7 Manual for
Beginners & Seniors

JERRY S. SPLASH

Dedicated to all my readers

Acknowledgement

I want to say a very big thank you to Maryanne, my wife and succor. She gave me moral support throughout the process of writing this book.

Contents

Introduction

The title of this book already gives a hint on what the book is about. It is a guide for new users of the iPhone 7/7 plus.

Dividing the whole book into three parts, the first part introduces you on how to get started with the iPhone 7/7 pus, the middle exposes a comprehensive list of tricks and how to execute them, while the last part culminates with useful troubleshooting tips.

Now, start savoring the content of this book.

SIMPLE, CONVERSATIONAL AND COMPREHENSIVE GUIDE

Setting Up The iPhone 7

STEP 1

Turn on the iPhone

The first thing to do on the iPhone is to turn it on. To wake up or turn on the iPhone, you just press and hold the Power Button. You should find this at the right area of the device. When you see the slider to turn of the iPhone, swipe it to the left.

STEP 2

Choose your language and region

The next thing you want to do is to input the information regarding your location. This will be the location where you are using the device from. This means that you will set up the language that you want to be displayed on the phone. You will also have to set the home country

Select the language that you would like to use and touch the country on the screen where you will be using your device from. Choosing a country does not mean that you will not be able to use the phone in a different country, it is just to set your 'home country' so hit **Next** to move on.

STEP 3

Connect to a Wi-Fi network and turn on location services

You will now want to connect your phone to a Wi-Fi network. If you iPhone is connected to the computer as you set up, this isn't necessary. But if there's there is a Wi-Fi network available when you are setting up your iPhone, select this and input the password if required.

That password will be remembered by your iPhone and you can connect to that same network anytime they are within range. To proceed to the next action hit the **Next** option.

If there is no Wi-Fi network available, you can scroll down to the bottom and tap the option for **iTunes**. When you select iTunes, connect your iPhone device to your computer with the cable.

After you have connected your device to Wi-Fi or iTunes, it should start to activate automatically. This will be in 3 stages

1. The device will show the phone number that is connected to it. If this phone number is yours, select **Next**. If it isn't, you can reach out to Apple with 1-800-MY-iPhone
2. Input in the billing zip code associated with the phone company account together with last 4 digits of your own social security number. Select **Next**
3. The Terms and Conditions should pop up now. **Agree** to this.

From here, you can choose if you would like to turn on **Location Service**s. What they mean by **Location Service** is the phone's GPS capabilities. This is what will enable you to get directions as you drive, figure out the restaurants nearby, find out movie showings around you and the rest of the things that rely on your location to work.

While it is recommended to turn this on, you don't need to if you don't want to. But you should know that if you don't enable it, many of the beneficial functionalities of the iPhone will be removed. So select your choice and proceed.

STEP 4

Passcode, Touch ID

This is that screen that lets you choose a security feature for your iPhone device. Of course it is optional and depending on your preferences, you may decide no to enable them. But it's strongly advised that you do. Even if you don't want to enable both of the features at least enable one.

For Touch ID, you have the iPhone 7 so this option is available to you. The Touch ID is basically a fingerprint scanner that is embedded into the home button. If your iPhone has the home button, you can use Touch ID. This will allow you use your finger to unlock your phone, to buy items from the App Store, iTunes or to pay with Apple Pay.

For Passcode, you will see the option to add a passcode. There will be a 6 –digit passcode that needs to be entered into your iPhone when it is woken up. If one can enter it, they can enter your device. It's a great measure of security and it is recommended to use it along with Touch ID

On the screen for passcode, you'll see the Passcode Options and this gives you a host of settings. You can select this if you want to change to use a 4 – digit passcode, set a password of a different length or use a pass 'word' and not a code

You will also get a screen telling you to choose your setup option. Do you want to restore a backup from iCloud or iTunes? Do you want to set up the device as a new iPhone? Do you want to transfer data from Android to the new iPhone?

Select your preferred option and move on to the next step.

STEP 5

Apple ID

The option to create an Apple ID depends of the options that you selected on the previous page. If you don't have an Apple ID yet, you'll be asked to create a new one.

If you a new iPhone user, you should know that your Apple ID is very important. So when you select the option to Create a Free Apple ID, be sure not to forget it.

STEP 6

Apple Pay, iCloud, Siri

The Apple Pay option that Apple provides is a wireless system for payment that works on the iPhone 7 and makes use of Touch ID together with your debit or credit card to simplify buying from many stores.

If you bank supports Apple Pay, you can follow the onscreen instructions to set it up.

The next stage is to set up your iPhone to use the iCloud related features. This is a free service that Apple gives to its users. When you have an iCloud account, it will be included with your Apple ID. Select Use iCloud and go through with the instructions.

You can also enable iCloud drive and start uploading files to the iCloud account you created. If you don't want to enable it now, you can just select Not Now

Siri is the well-known voice assistant created by Apple and you can use it to go through different options. It is here you'll decide if you want to use it or not. Select Set Up Siri to continue or skip with Turn on Siri later

iPhone 7 Tips And Tricks

What's up with the home button?

One thing is that the iPhone 7 does not have a real button you can call the home button. It's more of a sensor driven circle that's just like the normal touch screen. But there's a new option to use the Taptic Engine.

This makes it possible for the home button to feel more like a button when you press it. If you've used an Apple watch, you know what I'm talking about. You can still change it.

1. Enter the **Settings**
2. Go to **General**
3. Select **Home Button**
4. You'll find different options you can choose from to change the button feeling. Select one and hit **Done**

How about auto brightness

If you who use the iPhone 7 as your intro into the iPhone world, you would of course be wondering where you can find the toggle for auto-brightness. Your instinct comes into actions and tells you to go to setting, then display & brightness.

But you go try to go there but it's a dead end. If you want to toggle the auto-brightness option,

1. Enter the **Settings**
2. Chose **General**
3. Select **Accessibility**
4. Then **Display Accommodations**
5. With this, you'll be able to enable and disable auto-brightness

Taking a screenshot

If you would like to take a screenshot on your iPhone 7, you just have to long press the home button together with the sleep/wake button at the same time. When the screenshot is taken, you should see a preview of the image.

The preview will just show up for a few seconds after which it'll disappear. You can just tap the preview to edit the image before it disappears. When you take a screenshot, it goes to the Camera Roll immediately.

What of the lock screen camera?

There's this shortcut that we all love. It's the option to just swipe an icon when you are in the home screen and bring up the camera automatically. If you are confused about how to access the camera quickly, you just need to swipe left from the lock screen and the camera will be revealed. It's just the same process except, this time there's less noise.

Emergency SOS

While we don't wish to be in a situation requiring emergency, if you so happen to be in such a situation, you can easily summon emergency SOS with this trick.

1. Press the power key 5 times very quickly.
2. Slide the Emergency SOS across to call emergency Quickly.
3. Your current location will the sent and Touch ID will be reinforced so that you won't be forced to unlock your phone.

Force restart

Speaking of force, it's time to learn how to do a force restart for your device. There's no real home button for the iPhone 7 so the force restart method is not what it used to be. If you want to do a force restart,

1. Press and hold the Power Button together with the Volume Down Button at the same time.

2. Hold it down till the Apple logo comes up

The lightning port

When you get your iPhone 7 or the iPhone 7 plus, you should have adapter included with the package. With this, you will still be able to use your 3.5mm headphone jack instead of the lightning connector. But it's very easy to not to see this package since you're all excited to use the iPhone. You will find it when you take out the earpods.

Listen to music while charging

When you have your headphones connected to the lighting connector and your battery is in dire condition, you'll have no choice but to stop music and charge. But this just requires a different adapter. With a double lighting connector adapter from Belkin, you can't go wrong.

You get a port for audio and another for charging. How sweet!

Disable haptic

With your iPhone 7, any action will be followed up by some kind of vibration or buzz. If you make use of 3D touch, you get to experience it even more. This is called the system haptic feedback to tell you that your tap is recognized. To turn them off

1. Go to the **Settings**
2. Choose **Sounds & Haptic**
3. Then **System Haptic**

Control center shortcuts

Would you like more shortcuts to the control center to make life easier? If your answer is yes, you can do this when you

1. Enter the **Settings**
2. Select **Control Center**
3. Then **Customize Controls**

Raise to wake

There's the Raise to Wake option available for your iPhone deice. This just means that you can just pick your phone up and the screen will come on without pressing anything

1. Go to **Setting**
2. Choose **Display & Brightness**
3. Toggle on the **Raise To Wake**

Bedtime

Another feature you'll like try out is the bedtime feature. With bedtime, you'll be able to set the hours you'll like to sleep.

1. Open up the **Clock** app
2. At the lower part of the screen, you'll see the **Bedtime** mode
3. Select how much sleep you'd like to be getting's
4. Use the **Options** button to change the time or the alarm sound

Add more widgets fast

With the new appearance you get in the todays screen. With this, widgets are now more useful. If you want to add new widgets or edit existing ones, you just have to

1. Swipe left when you are in the lock screen
2. Move to the bottom and select **Edit** to find the other widgets you can add.
3. You can also hold down an app icon in your home screen so that you'll see the capabilities. A widget will come up and you just have to select **Add Widget**. You find this option at the upper right area of the screen

Use 3D touch

Ever since the introduction of iOS 10, there have been some massive improvements to the 3D touch. They work on older iPhones so of course they work on the iPhone 7 and 7 plus. There are many things that you can do with 3D touch but for now try to press hard on all app icons and notice what happens

For example, when you press hard on the message icon, the options for a new message will come up. You will also get a shortcut to view the persons you've contacted recently.

If you press hard on the Instagram app icon, you'll be able to reach the search, a new post, or the activity page. Also when the phone is locked, you can press hard on the notifications to get extra controls for that notification.

The hidden magnifying glass

You may want to zoom in on a very distant object. You can use your camera to do this but there's another option. It is the magnifying glass. But before you can use it, you have to enable it

1. Move to the **Settings**
2. Then **General**
3. Select **Accessibility**
4. Choose **Magnifier** and turn on the toggle for **Magnifier**

When you press your home button 3 times very quickly, your phone can become a magnifying glass. You'll also get a slider to control the zoom for the glass and a flashlight for dark areas. It's the perfect option to read a small text or doing other tiny actions

If for some reason the shortcut to triple-click doesn't work,

1. Reach for the **Settings**

2. Choose **General**

3. Select **Accessibility**

4. Then **Accessibility Shortcut**

5. Switch this option to **Magnifier**

Adjust the flashlight brightness

Here's another option that your iPhone 7 makes available in regards to sight. You get the options to control how bright your iPhone flashlight can be. This is made possible with 3D touch. Press hard on the flashlight icon and you'll get the option for Low Light, Medium or Bright.

Edit your Live Photos

With the option for Live Photos on the iPhone 7, you can capture a 3 seconds photo. It's something like a GIF. This was introduced in iOS 9 and it can turn your image into a moving photo. With iOS 10 however, you can edit those Live Photos. You can crop it, increase brightness or resize.

Use Touch ID for fast unlock

Touch ID, the fingerprint sensor for your iPhone is a great way to secure your phone. But it also has different options for unlocking. If you want to unlock the Touch ID, you either use a Light Touch or a Full Press.

If you don't like the default choice for iPhone and you want to change it,

1. Enter the **Settings**
2. Go to **General**
3. Select **Accessibility**
4. Find the option of **Home Button**
5. When you find it, turn on the toggle for **Rest Finger To Open**
6. After you have turned on the toggle, you really don't need to press the home button on your iPhone to unlock Touch ID if the lock screen is active. You just lay your finger

on the button. But if it is off, you would still need to press.

Lock lenses

If you use the iPhone 7 plus, this one is exclusively for you. We will be tweaking the way the rear dual camera works. You'll be locking the lenses. To do this,

1. Move to the **Settings**
2. Select **Camera**
3. Then **Record Video**
4. Look for the **Lock Camera** option and toggle it on.

This will help you not to switch between the 2 lenses at the rear when you record a video. Also when the lenses are about to switch, they can cause a flicker. Locking the lenses will also prevent that too.

Turn the keyboard to computer trackpad

If you are looking to make some changes to a document as you type, this trick will be very useful. It's the option to use the keyboard of the iPhone as a trackpad. You also get a cursor

1. Fire up an app that'll summon the keyboard, iMessage
2. Press and hold the keyboard and it will be empty
3. Don't release your hold yet but drag your finger around the screen to move the cursor.
4. You can press down on a word to highlight it or you can highlight the whole section by pressing twice

Get the lyrics

It's one thing to listen to music and hum the tune. It's another to know it actually says. With the help of Apple Music, you can display the lyrics to some of your best songs.

1. Enter the **Music** app
2. Choose the section for **Now Playing** at the lower area
3. Select the **Menu** at the lower right corner (3 dotted lines)
4. Look for the **Lyrics** option near the bottom and select it.
5. Now it's time to sing along. But you should know that it doesn't work for every song

Expand your view with landscape mode

Not many would use the iPhone 7 and Plus in landscape mode. In fact are you even aware that there's a mode called the landscape mode? Okay maybe you are, that's how you watch movies. But you can also use this mode for other apps so that you can get extra information regarding that app in one screen.

With Calculator, you get the scientific calculator. Keyboard allows you to get extra keys like the copy and paste or even undo. With Calendar, you get more details for the month, week or day.

Hunt down the criminal app

We all have that stubborn app that just misbehaves and sucks the battery. If you don't really know the exact thing that's draining the battery, you can just

1. Launch the **Settings**
2. Move to **Battery**
3. Move down and select an app. When you do, you'll see how long that app has been running in the background. When you find that it has been running in the background for a very long time but you haven't even used it, you may decide what to do with that app. You can uninstall and install again.

Use iMessage to mark up photos

If you use the Messages app to send a photo, you can also markup that photo. You just have to attach that photo to your message. When it is attached, touch the photo and you'll the option for **Markup**. Select this and you'll be able to draw or write with your finger.

Use the iPhone 7 camera as a QR reader

It's time your found out that your camera is also a QR code reader. You just have to fire up the camera app and point the lens to a QR code of any sort. The link should pop up in no time. It's a great option as you don't even need a third-party app to perform the function

Troubleshooting the iPhone 7

There isn't much difference between the iPhone 7 and the iPhones before it. But when you look closely, you will find that there are more improvements to the device. The two speakers and the camera are both outstanding.

But sometimes these features can begin to have some issues. If you ever happen to face any of these problems, this is how you can take care of it.

There is no service

When users turn off airplane mode on their iPhone 7, they may find that there happens to be no cellular service. Apple has made way to solve the problem but they also said that the devices affected were only a small percentage.

Solutions

1. You can try Apple's solution. Enter this link in your web browser https://support.Apple.com/en-us/HT201415.

2. You should also make sure that you have the up to date version of the iOS

IPhone won't charge

With the A10 Fusion chip and a relatively large battery, the iPhone 7 has a long battery life. But if the iPhone 7 doesn't charge, the battery will get exhausted sooner or later.

Solutions

1. The most common fault here is the charger. Try to use another charger to charge your phone. Alternatively you can use your charger to charge another phone. You'll need to replace your charger if you find out it has a problem

2. Have a look at the charging port of your device. If it's full of dirt and dust, then you know why it won't charge. Use a toothpick to get it sparkling

3. If it's not the charger or your outlet at fault, you may want to meet a technician

IPhone refuses to turn on.

If this problem happens, you start to wonder if the phone is actually dead. It's now that those who didn't perform a backup start to cry. Here's what you can try

Solutions

1. Perform a soft reset. By soft reset I mean, long pressing the Power Button and the Volume Down Button simultaneously for about 15 seconds. If you see the Apple logo, then it worked

2. If no logo, the device may be out of battery. Plug it to charge for some time

3. If that didn't work, you may need to Restore to Factory Settings

Black screen of death

The device is operating. You don't think it's on, you know it's on. But the screen is just black. What do you do then?

This mostly because of an issue with the hardware. If that's the case, then there's no easy fix for your iPhone. You can also try to do a force reboot. If that doesn't work then you should be looking to repair the screen.

No 3.5mm headphone jack

We all sulked when Apple said that they were doing away with the headphone jack. If you already invested in a sweet pair of headphones that needs the standard port to work, there's a workaround for the issue

Solutions
1. You should find an adapter in the box of your iPhone 7. You can connect the adapter to your phone and connect your headphones to the adapter
2. You can also try to get some quality adapters from Belkin
3. Go wireless. With the sweet AirPods, that's no problem

Poor battery life

The battery life of the iPhone 7 is of course better that that that of the iPhone 6. But some have complained about some rapid battery drain.

Solutions

1. Make sure you upgrade to the latest iOS version. The battery issues have been resolved there.
2. Go low power
   - Enter the **Settings**
   - Then **Battery**
   - Enable **Low Power Mode**
3. Find out if there's one stubborn app in battery usage
   - Launch the **Settings**
   - Select **Battery**
   - You can delete the app or update it

Poor speaker quality

Some have said that the audio from the speakers can be very low or sound distant especially when calling.

Solutions

1. Increase the volume
   - Fire up the **Settings**
   - Then **Sounds**
   - Swipe the slider for **Ringer and Alerts**
2. Ensure that the case for your iPhone is not obstructing the speaker
3. Check the side of your phone and make sure the **ring** switch is not in silent
4. You can reach out to Apple if nothing worked

No haptic feedback

This can be a bug with the 3D touch

Solutions

1. Try to restart the device and see what happens

2. Turn off System Haptics and then turn it on again
   - Go to **Settings**
   - Then **Sounds & Haptics**
   - Use the toggle for **System Haptics**

3. Turn off and on 3D touch
   - Go to **Settings**
   - Then **General**
   - Select **Accessibility**
   - Tap **3D Touch**

4. You can disable Skype's integration option. Some have seen success with this.

Device overheats

Users started reporting of the issues with overheating early on in the iPhone 7's lifespan. If your device gets hot when performing some tasks, it is normal. Like when you play big heavy games, use Snapchat and shoot a live video at the same time. You'll be pushing the CPU to its limits so it's normal for it to catch a fever.

Solutions

1. If it's a little too hot to handle, put the device down and leave to chill.
2. There could also be an app misbehaving in the background. Find the app and stop it.
3. Another great thing to do is to restart it. That's the go-to solutions for most problems.

Disclaimer

In as much as the author believes beginners will find this book helpful in learning how to use the iPhone 8/8 plus, it is only a small book. It should not be relied upon solely for all iPhone tricks and troubleshooting.

About the author

Jerry Splash has been a certified apps developer and tech researcher for more than12 years. Some of his 'how to' guides have appeared in a handful of international journals and tech blogs.